ADVANCED

SELF–
PUBLISHING
FOR AUTHORS

A GUIDE TO AUTHOR SUCCESS AND PLATFORM GROWTH

DALE L. ROBERTS

The Self-Publishing Manual for Authors: A Guide to Author Success and Platform Growth

By Dale L. Roberts

©2024 One Jacked Monkey, LLC

Paperback ISBN: 978-1-63925-038-7
Hardcover ISBN: 978-1-63925-039-4

Some recommended links in this book are part of affiliate programs. This means if you purchase a product through one of the links, then I get a portion of each sale. It doesn't affect your cost and greatly helps support the cause. If you have any reservations about buying a product through my affiliate link, then Google a direct link and bypass the affiliate link.

I dedicate this book to the memory of Walter Weyburn.
I'll forever miss you. Rest in peace, buddy.

CONTENTS

PREFACE 1

INTRODUCTION 3

PUBLISHING WIDE 11

MARKETING & PROMOTION 27

DIVERSIFYING YOUR INCOME 50

CONCLUSION 72

A SMALL ASK... 76

ABOUT THE AUTHOR 77

SPECIAL THANKS 78

ADDITIONAL RESOURCES 80

REFERENCES 82

Stay up-to-date on the world of self-publishing when you subscribe to my email newsletter. Once to twice per week, I curate and distill all the information you need to know so you can focus more on your business.

Visit DaleLinks.com/SignUp to subscribe today!

SELF PUBLISHING WITH DALE

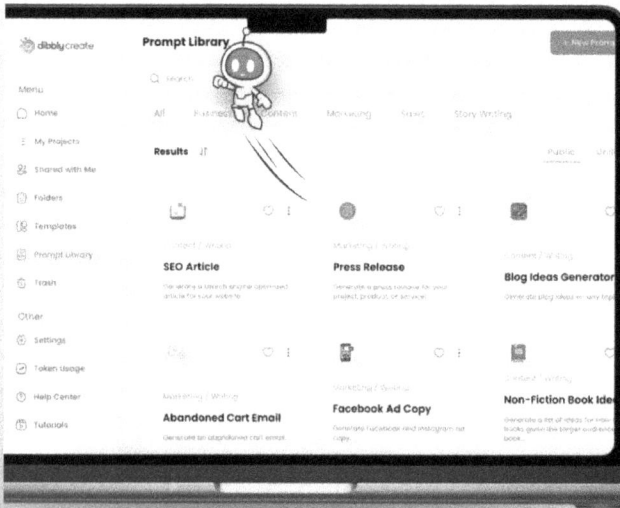

DRAFT 2 DIGITAL®

Next level tools to help you grow.

Whether you're an aspiring author or international bestseller, we've got the tools to help you publish faster, distribute wider and manage your business easier.

Learn more by going to **d2d.tips/dale** and read on to discover some of what sets D2D apart:

- ✓ Automated end-matter
- ✓ New Release Notifications for readers
- ✓ Payment Splitting for contributors
- ✓ Scheduled price changes
- ✓ Smashwords store coupons
- ✓ Universal Book Links via Books2Read.com

D2D 🖶 PRINT — It's print-on-demand reimagined.

Create a paperback on draft2digital.com from your existing ebook with just a few clicks, and **create a full, wrap-around book cover from your ebook cover**. It really is that easy!

Smashwords™ — THE indie bookstore.

your ebook. your way.

Massive annual sales, self-serve promotion tools, and the **industry's best royalty rates** of up to 80% list. Readers love discovering breakout indie authors at smashwords.com.

PREFACE

In *Self-Publishing for New Authors: A Guide for Writing and Self-Publishing Your First Book,* I walked newbie authors through the best first steps to self-publish. That book was just shy of being novel-length, but I didn't include everything an author should know to become a successful full-time author. It's hard learning this business alone as a beginner. Complicating it with more advanced steps would be like drinking directly from a fire hose at full blast.

Rather than bog you down with all the intricate moving parts, I gave you what you needed to know in Book 1 of the *Self-Publishing with Dale* series. Now it's time to introduce you to advanced strategies and approaches to self-publishing—strategies that will help you make more money, build a business, and grow your author platform.

This time around, you're going to take a deeper dive into self-publishing. While some concepts will include a brief recap so you have the foundations, most of the topics are all new and have not been discussed in my other publications.

I'm going to provide enough information to make you effective in this business while greasing your creative wheels as an author on the rise. Every strategy in this manual is something I have personally used and can confidently recommend as effective.

I wish I could easily hand off the blueprint to success, but your results will differ from mine. Based on your skills, mindset, and approach, you might get better, worse, or the same results. No, this isn't some FTC-enforced disclaimer. It's simply my way of being real with you. More people fail than succeed in this business. It's a sad but true observation.

But you don't need to be counted among those who fail in this business. That's why I wrote this short guide: to equip you with the right tools to prosper, even when times are tough. When your book sales are down on Amazon, they could be up on another platform. Or, if your book sales are sucking wind, maybe you can drive revenue through other sources like blogging, course sales, affiliate marketing products, and more.

As a modern-day author, you don't have to settle for churning out one manuscript after another, hoping to make a decent living. You can diversify your revenue and safeguard yourself against potential pitfalls. If you're the type of author who wants to write and publish simply for the love of the craft, then don't sweat it. I may not have much for you, but I implore you to consider some of these ideas.

The goal of this book is not to make you independently wealthy or to fleece readers of their hard-earned money. This book will teach how your writing creates a value exchange. When you build resources and tools and share them with your readership, you can give them more and get the same back.

Let's get on and dig in!

-Dale L. Roberts

INTRODUCTION

O ut of sheer frustration, I wanted to smash the Sega Genesis controller into small bits after losing for the umpteenth time in *Mortal Kombat*. I thought I was a more capable player than most people, but it seemed my dorm roommate, Brian, had button-mashing down to a science. I tried everything I could to best him—from two-finger tapping the controller to rapidly picking it like a guitar string—but nothing worked.

Sadly, no one truly enjoyed the game while playing with Brian. He didn't care about the fancy moves or button combinations that'd show off a unique ability. His only goal was winning. While any other person besting me would have been okay, he made it worse by gloating over each victory.

The sad part about it all was I also played *Mortal Kombat* for hours at a time and into the late night with our resident advisor, Paul. He just wanted to see his dorm wing happy. He didn't mind who won or lost. I could win and did frequently. I had fancy moves and button combinations, but all that went out the window when Brian came in, grabbed the controller, and then man-handled it with his rapid-fire controller prowess.

All the guys in our dorm wing would gather in Paul's room to play a tournament of *Mortal Kombat* matches. Each time, it'd come down to Brian ruling everyone and not caring what fun the game could be if he slowed down. Inevitably, though, Paul would intervene. While he wasn't one to boast or gloat, Paul won with all the finesse of a professional gamer.

My resident advisor did the fancy moves, the complex button combinations, and the best part about *Mortal Kombat*, the finishing move. He'd simply smile and then pass the controller off to the next guy. You can imagine my delight when Paul beat Brian repeatedly.

While you might think publishing books has little correlation with playing video games, you'd be 100% wrong. The business of self-publishing is like a video game in this way: you're either winning or losing. There are folks who dabble and just enjoy playing the game with no real investment in either winning or losing. Hobbyist writers are much the same in that they enjoy the craft of writing. Publishing and earning some profits are just a by-product of their work. Before Brian knocked me down a peg, I was merely that casual gamer—just looking for a fun time. After his constant bragging, I was ready to move to that next level—hardcore gamer.

Hardcore gamers can't stand losing and want to learn everything they can about a game so they can be the best. Those hardcore gamers are like the seasoned veterans in our business. They show how to succeed and establish a sustainable, long-term income through self-publishing with what seems like minimal effort. That's where most authors would like to be—generating enough income to validate their efforts.

When I broke into the self-publishing business, I treated it the same way I did video games. Constantly trying to improve and rack up more victories, I became increasingly frustrated with my results and constantly felt at odds with the other authors who were killing it in the business. I felt if only I could do the same things they did with the same finesse, I would absolutely crush it. Sadly, I needed to temper my expectations with reality. Subsequently, I gained insights into effective strategies, identified pitfalls, and improved the management of both my writing and publishing.

While I shared the fundamentals of this business in *Self-Publishing for New Authors,* this book is the next best step for elevating your author career. Though I make no representations that this is the ultimate guide or the most comprehensive resource on the subject, I'll give you enough information to get you going on the right path. That way, when you finally lay the foundation for self-publishing and are ready to scale it up, you have the necessary insights to make it happen.

Initially, you're going to be like my old college roommate Brian in that you've got one good trick, and that's it. While that's commendable and can score you victories, it will eventually leave you in one place for the long term. Given enough time and practice, you'll resemble my resident advisor, Paul, by winning consistently and making it look effortless.

Let's get to it!

THE FUNDAMENTALS
OF SELF-PUBLISHING

Gentleman, this is a football.

-Vince Lombardi

I n *Self-Publishing for New Authors,* I started with the very basics so new authors could get a fundamental grasp of the self-publishing business. I'm assuming since you made it this far, you already know this book is going to dive into more advanced strategies for self-publishing. If you don't know the best place to start or haven't even begun your journey in self-publishing, then some of these insights may go over your head.

Let's identify the best initial steps for self-publishing to pave the way for what comes next. Think of this as a brief recap of the last episode of your favorite TV show. Humor me on this so you understand the advanced concepts and why it makes sense to take these next steps.

Amazon Kindle Direct Publishing (KDP) is the best place to start for authors and self-publishers. KDP is free to use and has tons of resources online to guide you. They even have a course devoted to publishing on their platform called <u>KDP Jumpstart</u>. Though it only gives you the basics, it provides what you need to know to get started. Then, you can adjust as you go.

Publishing through KDP has its share of rewards and perks. Two perks include publishing ebooks and print books from one dashboard and having a reasonable payout structure. Not to mention you have direct access to publishing your books through one of the world's largest and most used online retailers—Amazon. Amazon earns approximately $28 billion globally every year through book sales, making up half of the Big Five publishers' sales and dominating 50% to 80% of book distribution in the United States.[i] It makes perfect sense why you'd want to start where the audience already congregates to build your readership from Amazon's deep pool.

Since its inception in 2008, KDP has exponentially grown and now sells millions of authors and their publications. While early competition for readers was lackluster, the game has changed considerably since then. The biggest issue for authors seeking to publish on Amazon is achieving visibility in a highly competitive market space. Another concern to be aware of is KDP's Terms of Service. If you run even slightly afoul of the rules, Amazon can terminate your account, withhold your earnings, and leave you with nothing to show for all your efforts.

Sure, Amazon KDP is the best place to start for authors, but it shouldn't be the place they stay for the rest of their career. Expand to other platforms to reach additional readers and new audiences. The sooner you look into the alternatives, the better off you'll be in the long run.

Never place all your eggs in one basket. Far too many times than I care to remember, I have seen authors hedge all their bets on Amazon only to be shunned for one reason or another. Amazon often leaves authors in the dark about the specifics of their alleged infractions. A few authors get their accounts back with a stern warning that sounds like this: "You know what you did. Don't do it again, or else."

Quite a few authors don't get that second chance and scramble to pick up the pieces. If only they had put a few safeguards in place, they wouldn't be stuck in a compromised position. The key to staying in business even if Amazon tries to shut your account down is diversifying. I don't share this advice with newbie authors because self-publishing is overwhelming as it is. If you're publishing your first book, stick with KDP for overall ease of use. But authors with a few publications under their belt and some experience self-publishing are in a better position to weigh the pros and cons of expanding their publishing options beyond Amazon.

It's a lot like juggling—the more items you toss into the air, the harder it is to keep everything off the ground. If you only add one or two items at a time to the steps you're taking to grow your author brand, then you better protect yourself against any one thing completely shutting you down. Should Amazon come along and deem your content in violation of their often-ambiguous guidelines, then you at least have a safety net in place to cushion the impact.

No one likes to think they'll have their KDP account closed, but it's always a possibility. Rather than put yourself into that spot, you can implement some best practices.

1. Publishing wide—don't just limit yourself to Amazon.
2. Marketing and promoting—don't rely on fickle search engine algorithms to deliver your books to your ideal readers.

3. Diversifying your income—expand your horizons and look into additional ways to monetize your author brand beyond books.

4. Tempering your expectations with reality—what you think might happen differs completely from what can happen realistically. Plan for the worst, and work toward the best possible outcomes.

The best time to diversify your author brand is shortly after you publish your first book through Amazon KDP. In a perfect world, diversifying wouldn't be necessary until you establish your brand. However, it takes at least two or more years to gain any real traction. Rather than wait for the right time, it's best to begin working your way toward a diversified author business as soon as possible.

Once you publish your first book through KDP, then you'll have a basic understanding of how things work and what to expect. As you expand your business, you'll be able to draw more parallels between one platform or business model and the next. It's going to be up to you to figure out those commonalities. I'd love to believe you'll have your light bulb moment right now, but you may not get that until you implement some of these steps. Don't force it; you'll get it when the time is right.

When you have your breakthrough moment, you'll find balancing multiple avenues and projects to be much easier and a little less intimidating. I'm not expecting you to do fifty thousand things. I will encourage you to continuously increase your workload according to your current skill set, lifestyle, and professional goals.

The best first step for diversifying your author brand is publishing wide. Rather than limiting your books to Amazon, you can reach a larger readership by publishing via multiple avenues. Then, if Amazon boots you from their platform, you have a backup, and your readers will still be able to find you. Let's get to know the best places to go and what to expect from each avenue.

PUBLISHING WIDE

When publishing ebooks through Kindle Direct Publishing, you have the option to opt into the KDP Select Program. As part of this 90-day exclusivity contract, your ebook must remain on Amazon only and cannot appear anywhere else online. This means your ebook cannot appear on your website or any other retail site. Once the 90-day contract ends, you will either:

- Auto-renew—which sets your ebook up for another 90-day contract; or
- Deselect enrollment—this gives you the option to publish or list your ebook elsewhere.

The KDP Select Program only pertains to ebook distribution rights, not print and audio book distribution. Your KDP Select-enrolled ebook doesn't affect the distribution agreement of the print book and audiobook versions. You can publish them wherever and however you wish.

Publishing wide means listing your title for sale on other platforms beyond Amazon. After all, every reader isn't simply camping out on Amazon to pick up their latest read. Heck, how many other retailers are there? Think about that! The options are nearly limitless:

- Online retailers
- Libraries
- Institutions
- Direct sales sites

Fun fact: Amazon doesn't distribute to libraries right now. While it seems baffling, readers still congregate in libraries. Though it's free to check out a book at a local library, authors can still make a living from sales made through the library systems. Staying exclusive to Amazon means your book misses the opportunity to appear in libraries.

Most patrons visit libraries, so they don't have to buy books. Sometimes, they use libraries to scope out books ahead of making a buying decision. Once they feel confident about an author or a book, then they'll part ways with their hard-earned money.

Though Amazon is the 200-ton pink gorilla in the room, they aren't the only ones to consider in the game. As big as Amazon is, they still don't reach every region of the world. Quite a few readers won't have access to your ebook if you stick to strictly publishing on the Amazon platform.

Admittedly, while I believe publishing wide is perfect for everyone, the reality is that it's not. Indie authors who use KDP Select get excellent rewards through:

- Page reads—Books enrolled in the KDP Select Program get paid based on pages read. Though it's roughly less than a half-cent per ebook page read, massive page reads can equal big paychecks. Not to mention, the ebook gets favorable placement in bestseller lists on Amazon, therefore garnering more attention.

- Promotional opportunities—KDP Select allows authors to use a 5-day free book promotion and a 7-day Kindle Countdown Deal (US and UK only).
- Additional advantages—Between the programs of Great on Kindle and Prime Reading, your KDP Select-enrolled title may be eligible for more love than those that aren't enrolled.

Sadly, these great perks aren't great for all authors. As mentioned, the per-pages-read payout isn't good, especially if you consider the low overall payout. Here's what that typically looks like:

Example 1: 1,000 pages read per day x 0.0045¢ per page = $4.50

1-Month Earning = $4.50 x 30 days = $135

Assuming your book is 250 pages, 1,000 pages are about four of your books read. Break down the $4.50 to the four books read, and you're looking at $1.12 per book. Most likely, those aren't just four readers because not everyone finishes reading every book. Though it's a killer deal for the reader, it's not so great for the author. I wish I could say most authors have 1,000 pages read per day, but very few probably see that many pages read in a month. That's the scary reality.

Some authors box themselves into the KDP Select Program and earn peanuts on the dollar for their work. If they remove the ebook from exclusivity, then they open more earnings potential through other avenues. Sure, they take a risk by stepping out from the comforts of the KDP Select Program. The risks aren't fatal and can be worth it if another platform pays more.

Based on the previous example, let's assume your ebook costs $2.99 and you profit about $2.00 per sale. All you need to do is sell one book per day on another platform to make up for the loss of income through the KDP Select Program. In fact, you'll make 78% more per sale versus the pages-read model. Sure, rather than reaching quite a few readers who may or may not read your book from front to back, you've at least got one reader who invested in your book by paying for it outright. They can read whatever amount without you receiving a penalty for the reader's failure to finish.

In the event you find publishing wide isn't yielding the results you expected, you can always delist your title and return to the comforts of KDP Select. Just be sure you fully delist your title so it's no longer available on any other platform before you re-enroll in KDP Select. Amazon has one hell of a system that crawls the internet looking for any titles that run afoul of their exclusivity agreement.

Popular YouTuber and indie author Derek Murphy inadvertently drew the ire of Amazon KDP (visit DaleLinks.com/Derek). He had a book published wide that he wanted to move into KDP Select, so he delisted the title everywhere. Or so he thought. One small random distributor fell off his radar, yet Amazon discovered it. After one stern slap on the wrist, Derek removed the title from the non-Amazon website and got back into the good graces of KDP.

If you plan to publish wide and then go back to KDP Select, double-check all your distribution avenues. It won't hurt to confirm the removal of your title directly with the distribution platform. It's a pain, but it's worth taking the time to do it.

Once you're ready to publish beyond the comforts of Amazon KDP, what are the best options? Should you go with one avenue over another? The account set up and upload processes are relatively the same from one distribution platform to the other. That's why starting on Amazon KDP makes it much easier when you decide to publish wide. Let's attack the next logical step for distribution: the four big alternatives to Amazon.

FOUR BIG AMAZON ALTERNATIVES

While Amazon dominates most of the profits earned by publishing online, millions in revenue are still available across scores of other retailers. The strongest players in the game and platforms that Amazon deems as direct competitors include:

1. Apple Books
2. Barnes & Noble Press
3. Kobo Writing Life
4. Google Play Books

How do we know these are Amazon's biggest competitors? Go right to the source. In *Secrets of the Permafree Book*, I shared how authors can set their ebook prices to free. By publishing your ebook to other online distributors and making it free, Amazon will price match.

But here's the catch. Amazon will not accept any old platform to price match. When I originally tested the price match method, I used the link to my book on Smashwords. Even though Smashwords is a viable self-publishing platform, Amazon doesn't view them as competition. As a result, KDP rejected my request to price match my book even though it was free on Smashwords.

However, once I listed my ebook through Apple, Barnes & Noble, Kobo Writing Life, and Google Play Books, KDP was all ears. The price match was nearly instantaneous. Amazon isn't about to play around. They aren't willing to be viewed as second best in the competition for book sales and distribution. When you mention any of those four options, KDP will take notice and honor your price match request.

Rather than going into detail about each platform, how they function, and what type of payout you can expect, I'll provide some general guidance.

All four platforms distribute ebooks and audiobooks. Outside of Barnes & Noble Press, it doesn't look like any of the distributors plan to distribute print books. Though audiobook distribution would seem like an advantage over KDP, getting access to the distribution is tricky. There's no direct path to audiobook distribution through two of the four avenues. You instead must rely on aggregate publishing platforms like ACX, Findaway Voices, Author's Republic, and more. Let's return to that topic later.

The compensation varies per publication type, ranging around 70% per ebook sale, about 25% per audiobook sale, and about 65% per sale of Barnes and Noble print books. Google Play Books recently increased their ebook royalty rates to catch up with the other platforms, and many authors couldn't be happier. Google's recent royalty structure update has leveled the earnings potential across all avenues.

Each Amazon alternative seems to sell best depending on the region of the world it distributes to. Should you live outside the U.S., you might find Amazon isn't the big dog in ebook distribution. In fact, if you check it out, Apple dominates the market share around New Zealand and Australia. If you live Down Under, then you should consider publishing through Apple.

Study your region and see where most readers purchase their books, then adjust accordingly.

Publishing to all five sites, including Amazon and the four big alternatives, is entirely at your discretion. I recommend if you're in for a penny, you're in for a pound. Go all in. If you don't take advantage of KDP Select, then use all the avenues. The biggest issue you'll find is managing five dashboards versus one with KDP. Yes, you'll have to upload to all four alternatives. Updating metadata and interior matter across all platforms can be a real hassle.

The good news is when publishing directly to all five platforms, you'll be getting almost all your earnings without having to worry about losing out on any profits. The bad news is you'll need to manage a lot of assets, and come tax season, you'll need to report all earnings from every platform. My accountant balances quite a bit in our annual tax reports, but it's her job to worry about it while I manage all those dashboards.

Should you want to avoid the hassle, you can always consider the alternative to the alternatives—a middleman, if you will. That comes through aggregate publishing.

THE POWER OF AGGREGATE PUBLISHING

The biggest issue with self-publishing is its accessibility—it's entirely too accessible. I know that seems wild to think about, but anyone who's been in this business for longer than a cup of coffee knows the options for self-publishing are seemingly unending. Self-publishers face a multitude of challenges with both Amazon and its alternatives among the Big Four Alternatives. Consider the other duties of running an author business and it becomes nearly unmanageable and somewhat overwhelming.

What if you could have someone handle distribution for you? Then, all you must worry about is writing, publishing, and promoting. Enter aggregate publishers.

The adjective "aggregate" means *to collect or gather into a mass or whole.*[ii] Aggregate publishers bring all the various publishing options into one place through their services. The way they get paid varies based on the platform. Usually, aggregate publishers get paid through a revenue share model. When you make a sale, they get a portion of the net profits. Conversely, they make no money if you make no sales, so they have vested interest in seeing you succeed.

Most aggregate self-publishing companies handle ebook distribution, while others include print and audio book distribution. Though I try to avoid playing favorites, I have platforms I prefer. It's simply a matter of taste. You'll have to decide what features you're looking for in an aggregate publishing platform and form your own opinion.

IngramSpark is probably the biggest aggregate distributor in the self-publishing space. Owned by Ingram Content Group, IngramSpark set up shop around 2013 to help indie authors publish ebooks and print books. Ingram Content Group has probably the widest distribution available since it reaches tens of thousands of online retailers, libraries, and brick-and-mortar bookstores.

In fact, Ingram has such a wide reach that even KDP uses them for the expanded distribution option of print books. If you want to get the best profits possible, go directly to the source and publish your books through IngramSpark. Deselect the Expanded Distribution option for your print book on KDP. The nice part about publishing print books through KDP is you don't have an exclusivity agreement to honor. You can publish your print book wherever you like.

The biggest barriers of entry when publishing to IngramSpark are:

1. Update fees—It costs $25 to update a book 60 days after publishing. Compare that to KDP where you don't pay a dime, and you can see how this fee can be a hassle. Later, I'll share ways to mitigate that cost.

2. Detailed metadata—The metadata–or the book's information—is more in-depth than KDP. Most of it is intuitive, while some features will leave you scratching your head and contacting their support line.

3. International Standard Book Number (ISBN)—You assign this unique identifier to a book, helping to track it within the publishing industry. ISBNs can cost anywhere from free to $125 based on the region you reside in. Currently, IngramSpark offers a free ISBN to US account holders only.

While the barrier of entry is higher through IngramSpark compared to the other avenues, the distribution and pricing control they offer is second to none. Not to mention the fact that you'll have the option to reach physical bookstores—aka brick-and-mortar stores. If you've always dreamed of having your book in a bookstore, then IngramSpark could be for you.

According to IngramSpark,[iii] simply publishing through their platform doesn't guarantee bookstore placement. To increase the likelihood of getting shelf placement, you'll need to offer a 55% wholesale discount and enable returns.

I won't argue over decreased earnings for bookstore placement. That's a choice each self-publisher has to make. If you enable returns for your book through IngramSpark, you're allowing brick-and-mortar stores the option to return your book while you assume all the costs. You'll have to pay for the print fees, shipping and handling, and any fees related to destroying the books. Instances of this happening are rare, but it's common enough to cause concern. If you can't stomach the risk or assume the cost of returns, don't opt into it. I feel it's not a gamble worth taking if you don't have a way to reimburse IngramSpark. What if a bookstore ordered too many copies and must return some of the order? You still must pay for it.

Yikes!

Other retailers to consider with a similar model as IngramSpark include Lulu, Bookvault, and Blurb. Lulu and Bookvault are two options I found to have great print quality. Lulu offers both ebook and print book distribution whereas Bookvault has plans to expand into ebook and audiobook publishing at the time of this writing.

The latest addition to print-on-demand publishing companies is Draft2Digital (D2D). Though the base cost of print books is higher than some platforms, it has an advantage for cash-strapped authors. If you can't afford an ISBN, print cover, or interior formatting, D2D has you covered. Any author who has a Word doc can get their entire ebook and print book formatted. No need for advanced graphic design software knowledge—just bring your own ebook cover and convert it to a paperback cover. D2D is truly a one-stop shop for most any author, especially those on a strict budget.

Initially, my biggest gripe with D2D Print was the steep cost of their print proofs. They have since dialed back the overall cost, providing options for authors of all budgets. When in doubt, reach out to D2D support if you're ever stuck and need a little help. They're a small, close-knit team of indie authors who are truly passionate about providing a highly accessible and useful resource to self-publishers.

What if you aren't looking for print distribution? What are other ways you can distribute through an aggregate publisher? This is where I lean heavily on platforms like Draft2Digital or PublishDrive.

For Draft2Digital, you get ebook distribution to some of the big four Amazon alternatives and a host of other avenues, including libraries and smaller online ebook retailers. D2D takes 10% of the retail price of your book. Though your profit appears to be 90%, it's much lower than you'd think. The aggregate publisher collects the money from the platform, then takes their cut. Since an aggregate publisher lists your title on different platforms with different platform fees, you'll get only a percentage of every sale.

For example, if you distribute to KDP via Draft2Digital, your sales will look like this:

Let's say the price of your ebook is $2.99.

KDP pays a royalty of 70%, so for each sale, you earn a profit of $2.09.

Draft2Digital will distribute to Amazon for you, but they pay you roughly 85% of the **net profit.** That means first Amazon will take 70% of your $2.99 sale price ($2.99 x .7 = $2.09). Of the $2.09

that you'll earn from KDP, D2D pays you 85% of the final profit. ($2.09 x .85 = $1.77).

Though you might think it's best to upload directly to each platform, remember you still have to:

- Manage more platforms
- Upload and update to more platforms
- Manage more tax statements
- Deal with the hassle and time of administering all those dashboards

Or you could simply let an aggregate publisher handle all that for you. It's truly up to you. I look at it practically. Should you make $1,000 or more through a specific avenue, then consider uploading directly to it. If you profit $1,000 per month in sales on Apple and Draft2Digital takes 15%, then you're left with $850. Draft2Digital is taking $150 of your earnings. It might take you less than an hour to upload and manage your title every month. Is your time worth $150 per hour? If yes, then deselect Draft2Digital distribution to Apple and go direct to Apple to collect all the profits.

If you are making over $1,000 per month through a specific distributor, see how much the aggregate publisher collects from the net profits. When dealing with a matter of $20 to $30 per month, then you must ask yourself this key question: "Is it worth my time to manage these assets directly with the platform?"

If it's not worth it, then continue using the aggregate publisher. If it is worth it, then go directly to the source.

To be clear, you don't lose any rights when using aggregate publishers. Using an aggregate publisher is simply for anyone who doesn't want the hassle of uploading to various platforms. Not to mention tracking down all the smaller distributors, only to find out they are inaccessible. Aggregate publishers work out specific deals that indie authors can't normally get on their own.

If you don't want to split revenue, you can always consider the alternatives offered by PublishDrive or BookBaby. These aggregate distributors take payment in advance, and then you collect 100% of all net profits. PublishDrive functions on a monthly subscription model, while BookBaby requires a hefty upfront payment for distribution.

You're taking all the risk while the aggregate publisher profits on the front end. Some authors can make this work if they have an established following with a proven way to recoup costs. I'd recommend being cautious when choosing these avenues. Once you list your titles through them, you're stuck with the platform. If you want to move away from their distribution, your titles will lose relevance in search engine algorithms, all the reviews will vanish from your ebooks, and you must start over again if you publish elsewhere.

AUDIOBOOK DISTRIBUTION—THE OTHER AGGREGATE PUBLISHERS

Because of the complexity of audiobook engineering and production, most audiobook platforms only distribute audiobooks that meet rigid criteria. Sure, you can publish any old ebook and print book with little worry about poor formatting. With audiobooks, you can't get away with that. Satisfying customers is the goal, so audiobook distributors have specifications you must meet.

The big dog in the fight, Audiobook Creation Exchange (ACX), is an Amazon-owned company that distributes to Amazon, Audible, and Apple. Though you are paid 40% of all sales if you opt for exclusive distribution, you must read the fine print of this contract. First, ACX determines the cost of your audiobook based on the total length. The longer books pay more money, so you'd better time it right if you want to collect a higher payout. Next, ACX will pay you based on the way a customer purchases your book.

Here's a brief rundown:

- AL—The Audible Listener credit is when a member redeems their monthly credit to listen to your audiobook.
- ALOP—Audible Listener Off-Plan refers to when a member buys your book with a members-only discount, usually 30%.
- ALC—À la carte is the purchase option available to non-members of Audible.

Thankfully, consumers have options! Now more than ever, indie authors can and should consider publishing wide with audiobooks. Sticking with ACX exclusively is similar to enrolling in KDP Select. Sure, you get certain perks like 100 promotional codes and a higher royalty. The biggest problem lies in the limited reach. You're only distributing your audiobook to three platforms (Amazon, Audible, and Apple).

In 2015, Findaway Voices launched a viable option for audiobook rights holders. Today Findaway Voices has agreements with thirty-eight different audiobook distributors, including distribution to some libraries. Rights holders are paid a generous share of 80%.

But remember, that 80% still refers to the percent you will earn of the *net* profits.

What if you want to distribute through both ACX and Findaway Voices? That is totally okay! You can publish your audiobook as a non-exclusive work through ACX. Yes, you'll earn a lower royalty rate, but your audiobook will be eligible for wider distribution. You can publish through both ACX and Findaway Voices at the same time.

There is an issue I need to mention related specifically about distributing to Apple: Apple audiobook reps have stated that Findaway Voices is a "preferred partner." When asked about ACX, the reps indicated that ACX was *not* a "preferred partner."

Also important to note is that Findaway Voices takes 45% of every sale made through Apple, whereas ACX takes 25% of every sale of audiobooks enrolled in the non-exclusive distribution option. With Findaway Voices taking 20% **more** than Apple, you will earn roughly 36% of each sale via Findaway Voices—which is 11% more than you would earn for the same audiobook on ACX.

The modern-day audiobook publishing model is still in its infancy, so I expect to see it grow in the coming years. While you have many ebook and print book distribution options, your options for audiobook publishing are rather scarce at the moment.

Though I am not endorsing these platforms, I can point you to Author's Republic, PublishDrive, Lantern Audio, and Audiobooks Unleashed as additional options to investigate. Every platform has its share of unique features and options. Be mindful of a few because they use Findaway (the parent company of Findaway Voices) for distribution. This means you'll be aggregate distributing to an aggregate distributor. If you publish an audiobook through a middleman who publishes through another middleman, then you will earn an even smaller slice of the profits.

If the aggregate distributor offers the option to deselect certain avenues (like Findaway Voices), then you can take advantage of them. Author's Republic offers three distribution options with unique retailers and websites. You can deselect the three options, but if you want to keep or remove a retailer, you'll have to contact their support.

PUBLISHING YOUR AUTHOR BRAND WIDE

Publishing wide applies beyond simply publishing your ebook to more platforms than just Amazon KDP. Newcomers may find publishing on multiple platforms overwhelming, which is why I believe it's not suitable for beginners. Once an author understands the business and how it works, then publishing wide is more practical.

Should you choose to stay exclusive to Amazon KDP and not want all the extra moving parts, that's okay because we have other ways to establish your author brand, build out your earnings potential, and grow your readership.

You'll be at a much greater disadvantage if all you have is Amazon, but that's not to say you can't make a substantial living through KDP alone. My fear is that you go all-in with KDP or ACX and get burned, then you'll find yourself with the smoldering ashes of your author brand. Build out your author platform, separate your eggs into multiple baskets, and better protect yourself from potential risks.

MARKETING & PROMOTION

Publishing a book and praying for the best isn't a winning game plan. No one will trumpet the arrival and presence of your book or brand like you do. Once you stop tooting your own horn, people will stop paying attention. If your name is Stephen King and you've penned hundreds of books with tons of movie deals, then you can sit back and relax. Otherwise, you're relegated to marketing and promoting your books indefinitely.

Between 2014 and 2017, I published over forty books in the health and fitness niche. Between guest blog posts, interviews, and featured website deals, my marketing game was on-point, and I had the sales to match it. Around 2017, I burned out and grew tired of writing about fitness. I finished talking about it in 2016, but I continued to push forward despite being miserable.

My interest faded in my fitness brand, and so did my online presence. Book sales dropped, and by 2018, my earnings were negligible. It was nothing I was proud of and something I knew I had control of, yet I couldn't bring myself to write another book about exercise to save my life. With a few sad attempts at marketing, I saw an occasional bump in revenue, but overall, the best days for fitness books were behind me.

The same will hold true for you. Should you ever publish a book and pray for the best, you'll find a lot of heartache and hassle. In order to be heard above the noise online and break out from the pack, you're going to have to do what others won't if you want to get what others don't. Marketing and promotion are never-ending tasks, and if you implement them regularly, you'll find a much better return on your time investment.

You don't always have to promote your book. You can focus on simply being visible as an author to build awareness of your brand. However, once you stop promoting either your book or your brand, then you're dead in the water. Never rely on search engine algorithms alone to find new readers and sell more books.

Though I deep dive into the subject of book promotion in *Promotional Strategies for Books,* I still think it's a good idea for us to spotlight ways to get your book out there and to nurture your online presence.

THE DIFFICULTY OF PUBLISHING WIDE & PROMOTING

The biggest issue you'll run into as an author with diversified assets is that you're going to have many irons in the fire you'll need to manage. For instance, if you publish your books wide, then you'll have many avenues to promote. While many readers buy their products through Amazon, you will find readers outside of the online juggernaut. With Apple, Barnes & Noble, Kobo, Google Play Books, libraries, and more, you have a ton of opportunities to find readers.

Where opportunity flourishes, however, you run into a big issue: managing all those avenues. While I recommend using aggregate publishers to distribute your titles, that comes with a catch. You have that much more to promote and build awareness around.

In order to do that, I want to start by talking about external sources that drive traffic to your books. Here is the problem. If your book is available on six platforms, in theory there are six unique buy links that readers will need to click to reach your book on the site they prefer from, for example, a social media post. Which platform should you send potential readers to? Amazon? Apple? Barnes & Noble? All six? That can get messy which you're creating social posts or sharing via your newsletter. Here's the good news—you don't have to choose just one. Let your readers choose.

Draft2Digital (D2D) offers a free service called Books2Read (B2R) that allows you to convert a single buy link generated from any platform into an aggregate buy link. All you have to do is drop your book's buy link into the B2R search window. Then B2R crawls the internet searching for your title and all the places it is available to purchase. Based on the sales sites it locates, B2R creates a universal buy link that includes all the platforms and versions (ebook, hardcover, paperback, and audio) available for that book. When you send people to this link, your reader can then select the avenue they want—Amazon, Apple, Barnes & Noble, and more. B2R sends your reader to the region-specific platform where they prefer to purchase your title.

Books2Read is a stroke of genius. You don't have to rely on multiple links or figure out which platform a reader doesn't like or doesn't want. The reader can choose from every avenue you've used to distribute your book, they can buy your book, and then the reader goes home happy. Simple and easy for both you and the consumer.

I recommend you use a domain name or memorable redirect to share your book quickly and easily. For instance, if you want to see where

Secrets of the Permafree Book is, visit <u>DaleLinks.com/PermafreeBook</u>. You'll see the various platforms available. Once you click a platform, you will arrive on the region-specific website.

In the past, authors would push their website at Amazon.com/ whatever. The problem is your audience outside the U.S. (buyers who cannot shop on the Amazon.com US store) are forced to search for your title. This creates more friction and diminishes your chances of a book sale.

You decrease attrition and increase the likelihood of a sale by providing your reader with a universal book link. If you decide to run ads through Google, Facebook, or elsewhere, you can drive traffic to the B2R link.

One last perk of using B2R is the ability to share affiliate links. If you're using Amazon Associates, you can use your ID in B2R. When a customer uses your link and buys your book, you get extra commissions for every sale. B2R doesn't take any money while tracking all the clicks for a given link.

Now, you're probably wondering, what difference does it make if I'm using one link to drive traffic to all the platforms? Well, if you prefer, you can generate as many links as you'd like. If you're running an ad on Facebook, you can have a devoted link for that purpose. If you're getting interviewed on a podcast, you can use a separate link. Once you get a good idea of where you get the most traffic, you can double down on your efforts for the platform where you get the best results.

No quick fix exists for marketing and promotion that yields instantaneous results for everyone. Once you experiment with different avenues and find what works, you can go back and do that consistently.

What if you're cash-strapped and don't have many options for paid advertising? Let's look at a few viable options.

PROMOTING WITHOUT A BUDGET

Regardless of your budget, I recommend starting with these low-cost promotional options. It's the path of least resistance, and you only stand to lose a little time and not affect your bottom line. As with all marketing and promotion, these promotions are a gamble, but at least when you avoid spending money, you're only out a little time. In return, you get exposure and experience. That's ultimately what you want—to be visible!

VIDEO INTERVIEWS

Start your marketing efforts with interviews. From YouTube channels, Facebook Groups, Twitch, podcasts, and more, your options are nearly limitless. While newbie authors will find landing the first interviews most challenging, more established authors will find it gets easier the more you put yourself out there.

Before you solicit hosts cold and blast emails out to everyone who has a YouTube channel, I recommend you research first. Search online for content that's best suited to your niche. I know this isn't as sexy or sophisticated as having a publicist, but I recommend you use Google. Search for videos showcasing your type of content. Once you find a channel on YouTube, Twitch, or elsewhere, watch the videos.

Keep the following questions in mind as you research:

1. Does the video creator resonate with you? If not, then no amount of exposure will help since you aren't vibing with the host.
2. Does the video creator have guests? If not, then you're probably wasting your breath asking for an interview.
3. Does the video creator do video reviews of books? If not, then sending out your latest werebear shapeshifter novel will do no good.

Once you watch and enjoy the content, then leave a comment or two. Yes, this will take a while, but you appear on the video creator's radar. I can't tell you the number of times I have had authors reach out to me for an interview on my channel. I had never heard of them, their brand, or their content. They literally didn't even care to know what my YouTube channel was about and what they could bring to my current audience. Those interviews were a no-go for me.

You can imagine how a video creator feels when people blindly reach out to them, hoping to leverage the host's audience to grow their own brand. It's not a good look for you, and it certainly doesn't feel nice for the video creator. When approaching video creators, remember the critical rule:

W.I.I.F.M.—What's in it for me?

It's not enough for you to give away free copies or share your insights as an expert in your niche. Show your dedication to delivering the best experience for video creators and their audience. Remember, the video creator took time, invested tons of money, and sacrificed a lot to build their audience. Now, you want to go in and take advantage of all their work? Not a recipe for successful low-cost promotions.

When reaching out to inquire about interviews, lay a little groundwork for the host by answering these four questions:

1. How do you know them?
2. What do you like best about them?
3. What value can you bring to the table?
4. Can you actively promote your appearance to their audience?

The last point may seem rather daunting—especially if you don't have an audience yourself. A video creator will feel more at ease if you're at least trying. I find nothing more defeating than seeing someone who appears on my channel who does no promoting and leaves me to do all the work.

Once you land your first video interview, I highly recommend posting it on your About page on your website. Brag about it and create a social media campaign showcasing the interview. It's pretty impressive to people when they see you're willing to step in front of a camera, be vulnerable, and get your name out there.

There are some authors you couldn't pay to get on camera. I totally get it. If you keep an open mind, you'll find it gets easier each time, and you'll see your author brand grow exponentially. If you are completely against getting on camera or don't have the tools to do it, then consider audio as your next alternative.

PODCAST INTERVIEWS

It seems everyone and their mother has a podcast these days. There's no lack of audio podcasts, and you can find just about something for everyone. Every single author can land a podcast interview. It's even easier than getting a video interview.

Follow the same steps: do the research and the outreach. Search for content in your niche and listen. Once you find a good podcast, collect the contact info from the podcast or their website. Do the same diligent outreach you did before. Listen closely and provide authentic details when you pitch a podcast.

Should you land the interview, make sure you clear your schedule, prepare well in advance, and make sure your tech is all dialed in for the occasion. You'll need a good microphone and internet access. Assuming all you have is a laptop, then the dashboard mic will be sufficient. Don't worry about buying an expensive mic or flashy equipment. Your host will let you know their tech specifications.

Again, once you finish the interview, push it to the moon and back. Don't stop promoting your interview. Making an appearance is like getting third-party credibility. Having someone willing to have you on their show is proof you are worth a second look. This will drive more potential readers to your books.

Add a link to your interview on your About page on your website and create a social media campaign driving traffic to that post. This shows how versatile you are and also acts as a business card for other podcasts. When you're searching for more podcasts to appear on, you have proof you're an author worth interviewing.

Side note: You'll find recommended sites and services in the Additional Resources section at the back of the book.

WEBSITE INTERVIEWS

This last recommendation is a bit of an outlier when it comes to interviews but can be beneficial for growing your author brand. Finding a website willing to interview you can be tricky. Once you find one, all you need is a little time to fill out a questionnaire. After that, the website host will publish it.

Much like video and podcast interviews, you'll need to build awareness about the published interview. While the website handles its own social media broadcasts and generates traffic for discoverability, you're responsible for driving additional traffic and enhancing relevance in search engines. That way, when someone looks for your name online, they'll trip over your author interview.

AwesomeGang.com exemplifies effective use of author interviews. Since their website is well established, boasting thousands in their collection, they have a ton of online traffic, so it'd be a good idea to get an interview with them.

Though we're talking primarily about free options, some sites do charge for a featured interview. Tread carefully into paid promotions and only invest what you can stand to lose. I don't think you should spend money on an author interview, but if you must, keep it to a minimum. For example, I published a video about marketing and promotion using Fiverr's freelance services. One gig included an author interview for only $5.00. That wasn't much, and I couldn't see how that'd break my bank.

If you're scheduling promotions on a very limited budget, you can always consider low-cost alternatives to get your name out there.

Then, you can leverage those appearances to land even more interviews elsewhere. Something is better than nothing.

GUEST BLOG POSTS

While some would have you believe blogging is dead, I can assure you it's alive and well. Blogging, short for web logging, involves sharing personal experiences online within your niche to attract an audience with similar interests. Blogging grows your online presence.

You can build a website and blog on your own. In fact, I highly recommend a website for search engine discovery. However, there are advantages of using someone else's website to promote your brand.

Unlike websites writing about you, guest blog posts are written by you for somebody else's website. You still get the credit, and you have another way for a different audience to find your content online. Much like video, podcast, and website interviews, you leverage somebody else's audience to grow your own.

You want to approach guest blogs in the same way as the interviews mentioned previously. Find out if the site accepts guest posts. You should also make sure your content suits the website's audience.

Rather than contacting the website and asking to guest post, you should instead come to the table with an offer they can't refuse. Put together up to three different blog topics based on posts related to their site.

You don't want to copy what they already have. Think about ways you can create companion posts that'll interest that blog's audience. Don't worry about writing the piece; you're simply going to pitch topics at this stage.

Once you get a website/blog host interested in your piece, ask what they specifically look for in a guest post. The article might have a required word count or specific keywords the host wants included. You'll also need to find out if they require any images or other content requirements.

A few best practices for making the ideal blog post and aiding with search engine optimization (SEO) include:

1. Length: A good blog post will be about 800 to 1,500 words. Again, confirm with the website host how much they want you to produce.

2. Keywords: Use a keyword relevant to your post in the title and use that term at least two to four times in the post.

3. Internal links: Since you're posting on someone else's website, it's a good idea to reference other posts on the website. This helps build cross-traffic on the site and cements your post as the go-to article.

4. Outbound links: Much like using internal links, you'll want to link to other sites away from the hosted website. Try inserting links to your website or other relevant posts involving you.

5. Edit, edit, and edit some more: Don't hand in an inferior first draft to the site host. It's a quick way to get rejected and lose an opportunity. Get another set of eyes to review your post before submitting it.

Guest blog posts can be time-consuming but can pay off if done consistently. Don't expect to see a ton of book sales. Focus instead on the long game. The more lines you put out in the water, the more likely readers will discover you and your body of work.

LEVERAGING SOCIAL MEDIA

While social media isn't mandatory, it's certainly an option worth considering since millions of potential readers congregate on any given platform. The toughest part of using social media to grow your brand is choosing the site that best suits your interests.

If you aren't too keen on social media, you'll need to lean on what your potential readers most prefer. If you're a young fitness author, then Instagram might be a good choice. If you're a business owner selling a product or service, think where you'll find business-minded readers. Sites like LinkedIn could be a good fit.

Pick one platform and stick to it. Don't bother with trying to be everywhere at once because you'll burn out quickly. Instead, choose a platform, study other successful people in your niche on that platform, then duplicate what you see working for them. That's not to say you should directly steal anything from them; instead, figure out what works for them and develop your own spin on it.

Having a social media presence gives you better opportunities than those without it. You can build a following and direct them toward your latest publications. The more you grow your audience, the better your marketing efforts will pay off. I often say nothing attracts a crowd like a crowd. Social media is no exception.

In my first year and a half on YouTube, I grew a following of 1,000 subscribers. Within the next year, I grew to nearly 4,000. After my third year, I hit 20,000. I'm approaching my eight-year anniversary on YouTube and have grown my following to over 95,000 subscribers.

At first, it'll seem like building a social media following is impossible. It'll feel like rolling a snowball uphill. The longer you push it, the harder it gets. Eventually, though, you'll reach the top of the hill and gain momentum in your favor. Stick with it and never give up.

Having a social media following is also a great way to leverage more author appearances and interviews. Once you have social proof in the form of followers, landing those interviews will be easier, because *you* will have an audience to leverage and won't need to beg for a guest spot. If the interviewer stands more to gain out of the deal than you do, that's huge!

I'm sure you can figure out how to find different social media avenues, but in case you're stuck, reach out to other authors in your niche. Find out what platform they prefer and any tips they can provide. You have quite a few options, including:

1. YouTube: Having a YouTube Channel has been helpful to me. The nice part about using YouTube is getting featured placement in Google Search.
2. Facebook Business Page & Groups: I believe one should not function without the other. Using your personal Facebook page isn't something I recommend. Set up a group about your niche, moderate it with your business page, and then drive awareness about your brand through the group without having to spend a dime!
3. X (fka Twitter): Even on the platform that limits character counts in posts, I landed some of my biggest interviews,

brand deals, and sponsorships. Here's the crazy part—I only have about 4,300 followers. Can you imagine the results if I grew my following even more?

4. Instagram: While this social platform seems to be dominated by fitness freaks and photogenic models, many authors have a substantial and engaged presence there.

5. LinkedIn: This platform is no longer the dumping ground for your resume. Since Microsoft acquired the website, LinkedIn has improved by leaps and bounds. Nonfiction writers especially thrive on this platform.

6. TikTok: I'd be remiss if I left out the short-form viral video platform that pioneered the #booktok trend. Many voracious readers love consuming books and sharing what they find with the world on TikTok.

While I could devote an entire book to social media platforms alone, I'm going to stop with this short list. It's enough for you to get started on any social media site. Don't worry about being perfect or growing a gigantic following at first. Just get on a platform and start making some friends.

PROMOTING WITH A BUDGET

If you have money to spend, then paid advertising might be right for you. The biggest concern here is how you use your budget. If you don't know what you're doing, you are more likely to lose a ton of money.

If you invest in paid advertising, go into it intending to learn and not with the expectation that you will sell books. Selling books is merely a byproduct of the learning process. Once you get some practice and learn how to leverage paid ads, you can slowly scale it and grow along with it.

The path of least resistance to paid ads is Amazon Advertising. This option is available to authors using KDP or Amazon Author Central. Also, Amazon sellers have access to ads through Seller Central or Amazon Advantage accounts. The issue with using Amazon Ads outside of KDP is you don't have direct integration so the reporting will be delayed on both the website and the ads dashboard. KDP account holders have direct integration to track pages read, sales, and overall return on investment.

Using Amazon Advertising, you can market to a warm audience. Compared to other advertising options, you don't have to worry if the potential customer isn't looking to buy anything. Chances are likely if the customer is on Amazon, they're receptive to buying something. Whereas with Facebook advertising, you're marketing to a colder audience. No one truly goes to Facebook to buy books, so it can be off-putting to some users when they see an ad in their feed.

Amazon ads have organic placement among other products. Facebook ads are more overtly promotional. I'm not punching down on Facebook ads because they can be quite profitable. But I believe the simplicity and accessibility of Amazon Advertising far surpasses that of Facebook ads.

Assuming you published through KDP, you can access the Amazon Advertising dashboard by selecting the Marketing tab. In the next window, select the region you wish to advertise in and select **Create a Campaign.** If you haven't set up a campaign before, you'll need to enter your payment information. Then, you're ready to rock.

If you published to Amazon from somewhere else, you may access Amazon Ads through an Amazon Author Central Account. This free resource is available to anyone with an Amazon login and books published on their platform.

Rather than walk you through building a successful ad campaign step-by-step, I'll discuss a basic overview. If you want to get a more detailed overview of Amazon ads, check out my recommendations in the resources section of this book.

When starting a campaign, you have three choices:

1. Sponsored Products
2. Sponsored Brands
3. Lockscreen Ads

Sponsored product ads are the best and simplest option for any newbie advertiser. The second possibility is relatively new and revolves around advertising an entire brand or collection of books. The last option isn't one of my preferred avenues, and I've found it to be a money-suck and horrible return on investment.

For the sake of brevity, I'll discuss Sponsored Product ads in broad strokes. When setting up a campaign, focus on a few key areas to get the best bang for your buck. This method will give you a better understanding of how to use the platform.

Set your daily budget as low as you can. Start embarrassingly low, so much that you wouldn't want to share it with anyone. This cost could be right around $1 to $10 per day. Don't worry, we do not intend to blow through that daily budget. It's merely a way for us to tell Amazon we can't afford to spend more than that.

Your next selection includes whether to use **Automatic Targeting** or **Manual Targeting.** With automatic, you're allowing Amazon to take the wheel and serve your ad to customers based on your product, its keywords, its categories, and any relevant products related to it. While it's not my preferred avenue, automatic targeting helps anyone new to Amazon ads to get their feet wet. Once your campaign takes off, you'll see what keywords and categories convert to buys. Monitor your **Search Terms** report once a campaign is live to determine what best converts to sales. Conversely, you'll find out real quick what keywords don't convert to buys. Slip those poor-converting or irrelevant keywords into Negative Targeting, so Amazon never serves your ad to those customers again.

My preferred method on Amazon is manual targeting. You're allowed up to 1,000 keywords per campaign. I recommend you limit your keyword selection to about 100 keywords. This allows you a little wiggle room and better ad management. As your campaign runs, you can grab high-converting keywords from your **Search Terms** report and then add the exact match to your ad campaign. Your ad will pick up momentum over time with every high-converting keyword.

Much like the automatic targeted ad, you can take the underperforming keywords and toss them into your Negative Keyword Targeting. The longer you have your ad out, the better it should perform. Remember, though, every ad has a shelf life. Much like a gallon of milk, you can only have the ad out so long before it goes stale. At that point, you can copy the ad or create a whole new one with the data you found in the previous run.

The Campaign bidding strategy offers three choices:

1. Dynamic down: This option means you want Amazon to

drop your bid if the ad placement is less likely to convert into a sale. Rather than wasting a ton of money, they're saving you some with this option.

2. Dynamic up and down: This option means you're flexible in your bids. It's only for experienced advertisers or anyone with a larger budget.

3. Fixed bids: This means you'll bid for a keyword only in the amount you posted in the campaign—no more and no less.

Only two options are what new advertisers should use: dynamic down or fixed bids. You shouldn't gamble much money on your ads until you fully grasp how the platform works. I recommend sticking with dynamic down, so you avoid blowing through your budget. However, if you want to stay fixed, then don't let me stop you. I don't know about you, but I like to save money.

Now comes the tricky part—setting your cost per click for an ad. Ads function via a variety of metrics but clicks drive the spend. We'll discuss more how clicks work in correlation with the other metrics. For now, understand that when a customer searches for a product or is browsing Amazon, they will be shown your ad. If the customer clicks on your ad to view more about your product, you must pay for it. Should the customer ignore your ad (see it come up in the search results but not click on it), you pay nothing.

Remember how low you set your daily budget and how I promised you'd avoid blowing through your daily budget? Now you're going to make sure of that by bidding absurdly low on your keywords. Do not use the Suggested Bid by Amazon. It's not a recipe for success, and most of the time, the prices are higher than anyone should pay if they want to return a profit on an ad. You're going to set your Custom Bid or Default Bid extremely low, and I mean as cheap as possible. I aim for around $0.11 to $0.16 cost per click (CPC). If you're feeling bold, you can always shoot for the lowest CPC at $0.02.

Before some advanced marketers host a book burning based on my advice, hear me out! The reason you're bidding so low is two-fold:

1. To not go broke. Keep in mind, if your book's profit per sale is $1.50 and your CPC is $1.50, then you're losing money with every click. That's just dumb marketing unless you have a proven sales funnel baked into the publication.
2. To pick the low-hanging fruit. While everyone bids absurdly high prices on popular and trending keywords, you're over here bidding low on keywords with less competition.

I prefer the second strategy when starting ads for a book. Once you find a few keywords at a low CPC, you can build keyword deviations and additional campaigns on the winning keywords. With every sale, you create more relevancy for your book in the Amazon algorithms. The more relevance your title has, the better opportunities you have when bidding for more popular and trending keywords. Then, you're not bidding stupidly high amounts on just one good keyword.

Once you have your campaign running, you'll need to monitor your reports daily to weekly. You're going to focus on these metrics:

- Impressions: This term refers to your ad being shown to a customer. The best part about impressions is that they're free! If you aren't getting any impressions, then your bid might be too low.

- Clicks: When a customer sees and visits your product page through an ad, it's known simply as a click. It's up to your product details to do the heavy lifting and convert a click to a sale. I hope you have a good book description; otherwise, you can forget any sales.
- Cost-per-click: Even though you set the bid, this amount can vary based on your choice of the bidding strategy. Monitor this closely and even more so in the **Search Terms report.**
- ACoS: Also known as Advertising Cost of Sale, this is a metric that helps you understand the profitability of your ads. Amazon will provide the ACoS number in your dashboard.

The biggest game-changer to the Amazon Advertising platform in the past couple of years is the **Search Terms** report. You can use this to get a better idea how the buying audience resonates with your product. I often find that customers give me better keywords to describe my book than the ones I originally considered.

In terms of what keywords produce the best results, you need to first analyze the performance of your ad once it's been shown to consumers enough times to draw meaningful conclusions. For example, if your product is getting clicks with no buys, does that automatically mean you've run a bad ad or chosen the wrong keywords? Well, we can't say just yet. We need to know the *actual numbers*. Just because you didn't sell a book based on one or two clicks doesn't mean anything is inherently wrong—the keywords, the ad copy, the cover, etc. You can't be sure with just one or two clicks because your ad hasn't proven itself yet. To determine any real statistical significance, you're going to need hundreds of clicks on that ad.

Consider this example:

Impressions = 1,000; Clicks = 100; Sale = 1

Assume it takes 1,000 ads served to customers to get 100 clicks. While you have 100 clicks, you've only converted one customer into a buyer. That's probably not a good ad, or you have some keywords that are eating up your budget.

Things look better in this example:

Impressions = 1,000; Clicks = 100; Sales = 20

Here you see a better return with one out of every five customers converting to buyers. This is a great ratio.

Higher numbers of impressions can help you better evaluate each aspect of the ad's performance.

Use this same thought process when determining if a keyword is worthwhile. Keep in mind, you need to look at the CPC and your net profit per sale. Therefore, you must bid smart and shut off a target that isn't returning any buyers. If I'm bidding $0.50 CPC for a keyword and my net profit per sale is $5.00, I need to convert a buyer once out of every ten clicks. Otherwise, I'm losing money in advertising.

What I have shared here about Amazon Advertising is just enough to make you dangerous. Review my recommended resources in the back of the book for a better understanding. No amount of reading and learning will replace what you'll get through experience. This requires an investment beyond just studying or theorizing. Just remember that Amazon ads will not work if you don't.

OTHER PAID ADVERTISING

Like Amazon Advertising, don't invest more than you can stand to lose. From Facebook, Google, YouTube, BookBub, Goodreads, and more, authors are drowning in opportunities to advertise. Many authors have had experiences from fantastic to fatal on each platform.

Quite a few fiction authors have found outstanding success running ads on Facebook, while other authors swear that Facebook ads are a money pit. Then again, I hear the same for most of the options out there. Know this: there's no single clear path to victory.

Pick one avenue and stick with it. You won't see any real traction immediately. Heck, you might even question yourself many times along the way.

As an advertiser, you must be willing to learn the process, analyze your results, tweak your approach, and continue pushing forward. When you don't know why an ad performs the way it does, reach out to the platform's support or network with other professionals actively using the same platform and learn from those willing to share their experience.

Always take any advice you get with a grain of salt, and that includes advice from me. What works for some authors won't necessarily work for other authors. Most of the time when I find something isn't working for an author, they're:

- Doing it incorrectly
- The method simply doesn't work for them/their genre/their readers

Always look at advertising like a business owner. If you don't get the results you're shooting for, then find out why. What do you need to improve? What should you do to mitigate costs? With time, energy, and attention, you'll see better results. Just stick to it, adjust as you go, and you'll find more success with paid ads.

DIVERSIFYING YOUR INCOME

admire authors whose only revenue comes from book sales. That's amazing. They only have to rely on their current publication and a backlog. It takes a lot of work and a ton of marketing to make that happen. While most indie authors would love to say they're successful at selling books, the reality is quite the opposite.

According to the 2022 Author's Guild Author Income Survey, the average author's yearly earnings sit around $10,000.[iv] No, I didn't mistype that and I even crosschecked the number. You could argue the report might not be universally accurate since it includes all traditionally published, self-published, and hybrid-published authors. In addition, it only covers a poll conducted across 5,699 respondents. That hardly covers every author.

In my experience, I have found that many authors make far less than that amount over their entire career. These authors often write, market, and publish over many years. While it's commendable to chase your dream and write for the sake of the craft, it's insane to be paid pennies on the dollar for your time.

It's easy for established authors and experienced self-publishers to tell you to just keep writing and that your day will come. The reality is you still have to pay your bills and hopefully see some return on your efforts. What do you do in the meantime while you wait for your day to come? Do you always have to suffer through lean times? No, you don't.

You don't have to pigeonhole yourself into being just a writer. You're so much more than that, and when you eliminate the stereotype of being a starving artist who's ready to die for your craft, you can begin bringing in a little extra dough to reward you for your expertise.

PAYING THE BILLS & BOOTSTRAPPING YOUR BUSINESS

In 2014, I made the naïve decision to bail on my perfectly good-paying job to pursue writing. With a hefty nest egg in a retirement fund, a decent savings account, and a few credit cards, I knew I'd be fine. All I needed to do was start writing, and the money would come raining down on me, right? Wrong!

Within one year, I'd burned through my safety net and was thinking this whole career in writing had been a bad idea. Thankfully, my pride got in the way. I refused to return to a day job and wouldn't go down without a fight.

My mentor, Jason Bracht, recommended looking into selling services through a freelance platform. He suggested I offer the services I'm strongest at, like video spokesperson, proofreading, ghostwriting, and anything else I could to earn a little extra money. Despite my initial reluctance, I gave it a shot and found the work pleasantly surprising.

The platform I used was Fiverr, and I excelled at video spokesperson and audiobook cover resizing gigs. It was baffling! I didn't even think anyone would care to work with me, let alone want these types of gigs. But within a few weeks, I pulled in a few hundred bucks—enough to help fund my book projects.

It worked out perfectly that I ordered book covers through Fiverr already, so I only had to use my account credits to buy my preferred cover design services. The best part was I didn't have to pay any service fees when using account credits, so I was saving more money by doing work on their platform and paying for the gigs with my earnings.

After my first year working with Fiverr, the earnings surprised me when I had to report them for my annual taxes. I had done enough work to keep myself afloat while paying for my passion for writing and publishing.

You can do the same thing. There are more opportunities than ever to offer your freelance services in various marketplaces. You're not just limited to platforms like Fiverr or Upwork, so do a little research and see what fits your needs best.

Due diligence is essential, especially if you want to get the best bang for your buck. For instance, on Fiverr, they take 20% of your revenue. Though that sucks, remember, you don't have to worry about managing a website, driving the traffic, or handling the money exchange. If that doesn't sit well with you, look into other avenues that may have lower fees. There will be a fee no matter the platform, so get used to it. It's the cost of doing business.

If you're dry on ideas, consider a few of these items for gigs:

- Ghostwriting: Though it probably isn't for everyone, writing content for other people can be a way for you to bootstrap your current book projects. While you don't keep the copyright of the work, you certainly get rewarded upfront. The buyer assumes the risk and pays you for the content, allowing you to carry on with your life regardless of their profitability.

- Editing & Proofreading: Not all writers are the best editors and proofreaders. Depending on your background, this gig might be a great fit. Stick with the types of writing you prefer to read. After all, if you're not familiar with romance writing, then you probably shouldn't be editing or proof-reading it.

- Beta Reading: Though this closely relates to editing and proofreading, beta reading doesn't require a keen eye for details but more of a big picture overview. You're taking a writer's work for a test drive. Again, much like editing and proofreading, state what niches you prefer.

- Miscellaneous: Think about all the things you do in your self-publishing business and how you can help other authors do the same. From copywriting, keyword research, marketing and promotion, social media management, and email marketing management, you could have a never-ending supply of freelance gigs at your disposal.

In lean times, rely on your resourcefulness and be resilient. In an ideal world, you'd focus solely on your writing, but when you need extra money, you must do what's necessary to stay afloat. That way, you can continue to write, publish, and promote your work. Don't worry. Freelance work might only be a temporary fix until you get your author brand off the ground.

BLOGGING ISN'T DEAD

Though we briefly touched on blogging earlier in the book, let's explore it a bit more. While many would-be experts would have you believe that blogging is dead, it's far from it. Sure, it requires much more work than it once did, but I can assure you that blogging is an excellent way to diversify your business and build your authority online.

Start simply with your author website when first blogging. When you're dry on ideas, you can always tap into what makes the most sense for your niche and audience. For example, if you're a nonfiction author, all you need to do is a quick Google search of your audience's most common challenges. Then, create a brief article supporting it. For fiction authors, snoop around your niche online and see what other fiction authors are doing. Once you have a good idea, you can always duplicate what works for them. No, don't plagiarize. Model elements you like best and make them your own.

Aim to write a post from 500 to 1,500 words with relevant keywords to the topic. Make sure your main keyword is in the title. Also, add any images you need to support the post and slip your keywords into the image metadata (also known as an Alt tag).

Ensure you have permission to distribute and sell any images you use, as simply Googling and using images you find online is not a viable option. To avoid DMCA takedown notices or legal issues, it's essential to use your own correctly licensed images. Numerous sites provide free Creative Commons images, but for a more secure option, consider premium royalty-free platforms like DepositPhotos, Shutterstock, and Getty Images.

Here comes the most important part—because you won't get paid without taking this step. You have a couple of options when monetizing your brand:

- Embedded ads
- Affiliate program

While I'm not the biggest proponent of embedded ads on an author website, I certainly think it's a step in the right direction if you need a little cash in hard times. Google AdSense has a program where you can embed ads on your site and get paid every month based on the amount of traffic you drive through those ads. To be clear, you won't be making a lot of money, especially if your site is only getting a few hundred visitors every month. That's okay because something is better than nothing.

My preferred way to monetize a blog is through an affiliate program. You promote products or services you happily stand behind and earn money when someone purchases based on your recommendation. To get signed up to an affiliate program, simply think of products or services you use, Google their name plus "affiliate program" to get details. The rest is intuitive.

Once approved for the affiliate program, publish articles that recommend the affiliate product. Then, when a visitor reads your article, clicks your link, and buys the product, you get a small portion of the sale. Not bad, right?

What if you aren't patient enough to build the platform and grow your audience on your website? It's time you leveraged other platforms to get more revenue. On sites like Medium, Substack, and, in the past, Quora, you get paid for your blog posts. I have heard many good things about Medium paying content creators well while the author builds authority and a brand. I used Quora's now-defunct partner program and saw moderate success. It wasn't the greatest payday, but I got enough money for the effort to be worthwhile.

You can also consider other avenues to post blogs, including LinkedIn, Facebook, Tumblr, and beyond. Though these platforms don't have a readily available monetization program for blogging, it's certainly a website you can leverage to grow your audience. Do I prefer using these avenues? No, but it certainly is an alternative to building out a blogging website from scratch.

VIDEO RULES THE INTERNET

If I didn't make it clear enough in the previous chapter, I think it's high time you get a clear understanding of why video is the most effective tool in your arsenal.

In 2022, 82% of online traffic came from video streaming and downloads.[v] While most authors would rather crank out their next manuscript, the savvy author spends a little extra time building an online presence through video. Though video stands in direct defiance of the stereotypical author—isolated and introverted—it can be one the best things you can take on right now. I've seen many authors over the years who used video to build out their brand only to find their video presence took off faster than their publications.

One hand washes the other. When your video presence grows, so will your book sales, and vice versa.

Meanwhile, you could get paid for your efforts through various monetization programs. Right now, YouTube is the king of all online videos. Owned by Alphabet—the same company that owns Google—this video hosting platform is here to stay. While you won't earn any real money starting out, you can still monetize your efforts through some of the other vehicles mentioned later in this chapter.

The YouTube Partner Program is how video creators monetize their efforts on the video hosting site. Currently, to be eligible for the YouTube Partner Program, you must have 1,000 subscribers and 4,000 watch time hours within one rolling year. YouTube also accepts 10,000,000 views of short-form videos in the last 90 days as an alternative to the 4,000 watch time hours. Once approved, you can then allow YouTube to run ads on your videos in one of many ways, including:

1. Pre-, mid-, and post-roll ads: You allow YouTube to put an ad at the beginning, middle, and end of your videos. While you need to have at least eight minutes of content for mid-roll ads, you don't have any pre- and post-roll ad limitations.
2. Various placements: Overlays, sidebars, and other ads are placed on your video.

To be clear, you won't have a say about who advertises on your videos. Sure, you can block specific websites through Google AdSense, but you won't know who is serving an ad on your video unless a viewer tells you or you see it.

Another way to access the YouTube Partner Program is with 500 subscribers, three video uploads in the last 90 days, and 3,000 watch time hours in the last year. You get access to monetization tools like Channel Memberships, Super Chats, Super Stickers, and Super Thanks—crowdfunding tools that all video creators get in the YouTube Partner Program. While this entry point won't give you the option to run ads, it's a great starting point for growing your brand without going broke.

A great example of an author who saw the value is an old pal, Walter Weyburn. Early in his self-publishing career, Walter crushed it in self-publishing. He was publishing one hit after the other. One day, it all ended. His revenue dried up, and Walter ran out of options. Naturally, he took to YouTube and shared some of his insights into self-publishing.

Through private conversations, Walter shared his frustrations with self-publishing and the lack of movement on YouTube. I calmly assured him that YouTube is a long game. Just as he was ready to give up, Walter hit a breakthrough. Literally, in a month, his YouTube channel became monetized, and his financial dry spell ended.

Since his channel exploded practically overnight, more people flocked to his videos, more ads came up, and Walter got paid for his efforts. Indirectly, he grew his presence as an author and an authority in his niche. His channel hit over 100,000 subscribers in one year, drove hundreds of thousands of views, and earned a hefty paycheck every month.

Will you have the same success Walter has? Possibly, but you won't know unless you give it the old college try. And the most important part is to never give up under any circumstances. Quite a few people

I know within the video creator community are like Walter and earn enough revenue from YouTube to make a decent living. But that took time, attention, energy, and perseverance.

In the meantime, if you can't make money from the YouTube Partner Program or join any other monetization program with Twitch, TikTok, or the like, then you need to consider the quicker victories. Though it requires a little upfront work and time, you can earn extra cash to make it a bit more worthwhile.

CREATE AN ONLINE COURSE

You're a creative entrepreneur; otherwise, you wouldn't be writing and publishing your work. With this creativity comes a special set of skills and insights. Other people would kill to know what you know, so rather than make someone stand trial for homicide, why don't you give them what they want for a small fee?

Online course creation seems a little overwhelming and, sometimes, a bit of a stretch if you've never done one before. I assure you it can be a good fit for all authors as long as you take the time to know your audience and their needs.

Nonfiction authors have it the easiest. Publishing reality-based work makes you a bit of an expert in your field. At a minimum, you're a curator with deep insights into your niche.

It'd be nice to think everyone will buy all your books, but the truth is not everyone has the discretionary time or patience to read them. Why not make matters easy by putting your expertise into a simple step-by-step program broken down for your audience? Building out a course like this allows you to continue promoting and sharing your publications. Courses act as another promotional tool to grow your brand and sell more books.

Keep in mind that you'll be able to leverage courses in other ways and not just more revenue and book sales. We'll get to another method in just a moment.

For now, let's address the pesky elephant in the room: what about fiction authors? How are fiction authors supposed to create a course if all they've done is build out imagined realms? That's it right there! Your creativity and insights as a fiction author are second to none. While you might think it's second nature or nothing worthwhile, many aspiring authors crave to know what you do to produce better manuscripts.

My good friend Michael La Ronn of the YouTube channel Author Level Up is a prime example of a fiction author producing nonfiction content and courses. Michael launched a case study based on his experience of breaking ground in a new genre. At first, he allowed members in for free to test out the beta version. Once he completed the course on building a new author brand in a different niche, Michael then charged for admission. I can't speak about how much Michael made in course sales, but I'm confident he pulled in enough revenue to make it worthwhile for everyone.

As a fiction author, share your whole writing process, including character development, world-building, and more. Your only limit is your imagination on course creation. Since you're a fiction author, I think it isn't much of a stretch for you to create a course.

As you plan your course, I want you to think about additional ways to derive revenue from your course content. Sounds difficult, right? Well, it's not.

COACHING & CONSULTS

Sometimes people don't want to bother with reading books or going through a course. They simply want to get the information directly from the horse's mouth. If you're an expert in your field, then chances are likely someone will pay a premium to learn right from you.

There are two ways people can learn: the easy way and the hard way. With the hard way, people have to consume the information, take time to learn it, implement what they learn, adjust course, and repeat. When doing it the easy way, people can pay a premium to skip to the front of the line. Why learn everything the hard way when you can have an expert guide you through the process, steer you away from pitfalls, and help you reach success faster than if you'd done it on your own?

While coaching and consulting aren't for everyone, it's certainly an option worth entertaining. If you don't want to bother with creating a course, then coaching and consulting might be for you. If you have a course created, consider using coaching and consulting as an upsell or alternative revenue stream.

Since consultations require more of your time, ask for a higher investment from your customer. Remember that you didn't learn what you know overnight. You didn't just wake up one day and become an expert. Also, you're taking time out of your day to devote to somebody else. What happens while you're working with somebody else? Do your everyday affairs go on hold, or do you have to have outsource your normal activities?

Put together realistic rates for your consultations. You may have to use a payment processor like PayPal to accept money. If you book up your time, then start charging more. It's all about supply and demand. If you have little time, then you need to charge more. Your time is precious, so make it worthwhile for you and your client.

AFFILIATE MARKETING FOR THE WIN

About four years ago, I stumbled over a YouTube channel hosted by Dan Brock, the Deadbeat Super Affiliate. His approach was comical, yet his results were real. Dan shared the power of affiliate marketing—where you promote or advertise a product or service in exchange for a portion of the sales.

I didn't know where to begin. After all, who would really want to buy a product or service based on my recommendation? I wasn't anyone special, and why would a stranger trust me? Yet through his teachings, Dan shared this adage:

If you build it, they will come.

I scoured various online forums, affiliate marketing websites, and videos, yet I still came up empty-handed. How would I ever be able to make any substantial money in affiliate marketing if I couldn't find a product that fit my needs?

This was right around the time I was first growing my YouTube channel, so you can imagine how my ears perked when Dan said video was a great avenue to share affiliate products. Just a simple review, product demonstration, or testimonial would work. Still, I encountered challenges finding something I could support wholeheartedly without jeopardizing the trust I had gained from my small YouTube fanbase.

I shared my frustration with my wife, Kelli, and she chimed in on something that changed the trajectory of my career on YouTube and in affiliate marketing.

"You like Grammarly so much, why don't you do a review video?" she asked.

"Really? Who'd even care about my opinion about Grammarly?" I wondered if it'd even make sense to share my love for the online grammar-checking tool.

Rather than get hung up on another product, I pulled the trigger. Within the first month, the Grammarly video pulled in thousands of views. For every 100 views, someone clicked my affiliate link. While Grammarly paid cents on the dollar for free account holders, they paid a premium for anyone who upgraded. After a few months, I pulled in hundreds in revenue from Grammarly and additional money through Google AdSense.

Thankfully, I listened to my wife and followed her instructions. Since then, I have created dozens of affiliate marketing videos and got better at the presentations. With every video getting better, the revenue increased. I saw affiliate marketing could be an entirely different way to make a living beyond writing.

As mentioned previously, to find the best affiliate marketing programs, search for your favorite brand, product, or service. It helps if you already use the product. Sure, you can find opportunities through platforms like Clickbank or Warrior Plus, but those products are a little less mainstream and can sometimes fall a little short of your expectations. If you use a product from those sites, then promote it.

Just make sure if you promote any product, you:

- Only promote something you can truly get behind
- Fully disclose the nature of your participation in the affiliate program

With the latter point, you can simply state it in the video or on a written post. The disclosure prevents you from getting beat up with FTC fines or blacklisted. Also, it lets people know you stand something to gain by sharing the product. Don't worry about trolls and people who think you're just in it for the money. An old friend once said to me:

You can never say the right thing to the wrong person, and you never say the wrong thing to the right person.

You don't have to sweat the people who try to punch you down for endorsing a product. Sure, you stand to gain something out of the sale, but it doesn't make you any less of a person. Keep pushing forward and share products you like so you can get paid in the process.

Think of when a friend has recommended a movie or shared a bargain at a local store. That friend never got paid a dime for sharing it while the movie theater or store made all the money. Imagine if that wasn't such a one-sided transaction. What would happen if your friend received a reward for sending you there? You'd probably enjoy repaying a friend for doing something you'd do anyway. That's the benefit of affiliate marketing.

Affiliate marketing extends beyond video. Before you promote a product, familiarize yourself with the Terms of Service for each affiliate program. Some programs have quite a few do's and don'ts that you will need to abide by or stand to lose your earnings.

For instance, the Amazon Associates program forbids link sharing in publications and emails. Amazon prefers you share the link on your website or social media. Meanwhile, you must fully disclose the nature of the link. With other affiliate programs, you cannot run ads on specific keywords related to the product.

Once you understand that you must review each affiliate program's Terms of Services, you can consider other potential ways to share the product. Here are a few:

1. Books: Of course, share affiliate products in a book. Again, fully disclose it in your book on the copyright page or in the content. For instance, can you spot all the affiliate products I mention in this book?

2. Videos: Take a page out of my playlist and create a review, demonstration, or overview video of a product. It doesn't need to be perfect. Heck, on another channel I manage, I have a cheesy video showing the Iron Gym Pull-Up Bar. Though the channel isn't in the YouTube Partner Program, I still get commissions from the sales generated through the video.

3. Social Media: Facebook, Instagram, TikTok, Twitter, and more are places for you to share your love for a product.

4. Blogging: Produce an interesting article that highlights the features of your preferred affiliate product.

Though these are just a few options, you have many other avenues to consider. Think about all the ways people find you and leverage those avenues.

LANDING SPONSORSHIPS & BRAND DEALS

As your brand grows, you will reach more people. With that reach, many companies will want to work with you beyond simply affiliate marketing programs. Enter sponsorships and brand deals!

When a company wants to gain more exposure beyond traditional methods—TV, video ads, magazines, and newspapers—they lean on influencer marketing. Now, hear me out before you say, "Nope, Dale. I'm not an influencer, and I don't plan on being one."

You're in the business of writing and publishing books. Therefore, you want people to read your books. You evoke an emotional response from your reader. Maybe they get a specific outcome from using the tips in your nonfiction book. Perhaps they get inspired by your uplifting young adult romance novel. Either way, you influence your readers.

Boom! Hopefully, you just realized that everyone is an influencer. It's not a dirty word, and you should learn to embrace it.

Now, I'm not telling you to go around and tell anyone you're a full-time influencer because they'll think you're a complete narcissist and egomaniac. What I am telling you is you have more opportunities beyond the previously mentioned monetization avenues.

The tricky part is knowing when the right time is to get sponsorships or brand deals. This really comes down to the direction you're taking your author brand. If you know the marketing and promotional strategies that'll grow your brand, it's much easier to seek out sponsorships and brand deals.

Almost anyone can land a sponsorship or brand deal with a few best practices in place. This includes:

- Prospecting: Yes, you must reach out to brands and companies you believe will best fit your author brand.
- Professional appearance: Create a professional press kit with relevant information about you, including your social media following, your publications, your awards, and any other insights. See my four-time award-winning book, *Promotional Strategies for Books.*
- Proposal: Create an offer they can't refuse. Pitch companies on how you can best serve their needs with your current readership or community.
- Following up: Most companies will need time to process a proposal and will sometimes need a gentle reminder of your potential deal.
- Payment processing: Accepting cash or checks is a recipe for disaster. You'll need a good payment processor in place before finalizing your agreement.

If you want to land a deal, you're going to need to do some outreach. Remember how you searched for affiliate marketing programs? Prospecting works much in the same way. Do a simple search of the company and look for how to contact them. Most companies or brands have a **Contact Us** page with a web form or an email address.

Keep your dialogue brief and don't overwhelm them with details. The best way to approach it is by sharing who you are and what you bring to the table. What unique value do you offer they can't achieve on their own? Once you can answer that question, you'll be able to approach almost any company. Now, don't be mistaken. You're going to get a lot of rejections at first. In due time, you'll find a company that'll say yes.

To be clear, the first communication should not include your proposal. The first outreach should be about discovery. You can simply ask:

Who do I need to contact about sponsorships?

All you're looking for is a foot in the door and a person to talk to. Once you get a contact, reach out to them. Do not wait. Turnover happens in companies, so you don't want to wait only to find out your contact has left the company already. Once you connect with the company contact, be brief again. Introduce who you are and what they stand to gain from a sponsorship with you.

I prefer setting up a video chat with the company spokesperson since I believe people connect better face-to-face. Though I can set up a brand deal through email, the likelihood of rejection is greater. After all, the person on the other end of the conversation will feel less connected to you and will focus more on the dollar amount on a proposal. Whereas on a video chat, I can express the value of the deal and communicate the value attached to the agreement more effectively.

How you communicate with the company spokesperson is up to you. If you don't feel comfortable on camera, then stick with email. Conversely, if you shine on camera, then video chats might be for you.

The sponsorships and brand deals you're most likely to land are with people you already know. Otherwise known as warm prospects, established connections in your network can be a great way to get your feet wet in the world of sponsorship deals. It's also easier to hear a "no" from someone you know than a stranger. Once you get the rejection, you can always ask why or how you could've better approached the deal. This criticism is great for developing future proposals and forming relationships with companies.

The next million-dollar question is how do you present a proposal? It doesn't have to be too fancy. In fact, I conducted my first deals simply by creating a PDF on Microsoft Word. Later, I used Canva to create eye-catching graphics and a proposal that made the company spokesperson take note. However, I really grabbed attention when I invested in proposal services like Nusii and Quoters (see the Resources).

Though the proposal services cost a premium, I more than got a return on my investment after the first deal. Proposal services excel in what they do for a reason, so paying for them is a simple decision. You can use templates, fill in costs, add in brand-specific details, and arrange payment directly through the platform.

My final bit of advice regarding sponsorship deals and proposals will require a little extra investment upfront. Consult a lawyer. You'll need to put together a deal that doesn't leave you high and dry should the sponsors want to back out or cry foul on the deliverables. Get all the bases covered so you do not get duped.

Once you send the proposal, ask when the best time is to follow up. If you get a "we'll contact you," then the chances are likely that deal won't happen. When they share the best time to contact them, you must treat it like an appointment. Follow up with your contact and cover every question and concern. Look for the solid yes or no. If you get a no, find out if it's a "not right now" or a firm "no."

Do not personalize the rejection. Find out what you could've done better to address the company's concerns. Their reasons can vary from a lack of budget to not seeing enough value in the agreement. Address those issues and see if they will negotiate. Just remember, when negotiating, don't undersell yourself or offer bargain-basement pricing.

Should a company accept your proposal, then it's time to arrange payment. Look into payment processing companies like PayPal or Stripe. Though both companies collect a fee per transaction, it's worth the cost to handle the processing. You can report any fees incurred from a payment processor as a tax write-off annually. Whatever company you choose for payment processing needs to be quick, easy, and universally recognized. Companies feel confident using a familiar payment service.

When collecting payments, I recommend requiring a 50% deposit before you start any work. That upfront investment makes the company less likely to flake out and bail on you after you have delivered the work. I always require full payment of the sponsorship money before delivering the goods. I look at it like a fast-food restaurant—you don't get your food and then pay. You pay and then get your food. How you accept sponsorship money is up to you, but remember, you stand to lose a lot more by not having some compensation in advance.

When putting together your proposal, be sure you're clear on what you will and won't do. I've heard horror stories of people securing dream sponsorships, only to have every detail tightly controlled and micromanaged. Most of my sponsorship agreements revolve around my YouTube channel, with deliverables tied to on-camera activities. I refuse to do business with a company that wants me to compromise my message or change my content beyond what I normally do.

Last, base how much you charge the company on what you perceive as the best value you bring to the table. Figure out what the company gains from working with you and leveraging your audience. Then, whatever their outcome, divide the profits meaningfully. Determining an ideal sponsorship dollar amount comes down to guesswork at first. Eventually, you'll know what makes for a winning situation—for you, the company, and your audience.

If your sponsorship deliverables don't live up to expectations, the company will let you know in one of two ways: they'll tell you, or they'll reject future proposals. Don't take it personally. Learn from it, adjust course, and move on. If I see a deal hasn't fared as well as I would've liked, then I try to make it good with the company. This could include delivering something extra like an email broadcast, social media campaign, or shout-out on-air.

Sponsorships and brand deals can be the most rewarding of all the monetization avenues. You align with a company you already like while being paid. This compensation goes above and beyond simply the risk of affiliate marketing, where you hope someone buys based on your influence.

CONCLUSION

When I first broke into the business of self-publishing in 2014, I truly believed I would replace the full-time income from my day job immediately. In reality, that didn't happen for another few years. It was defeating and a blow to my ego when I didn't get results I thought I could. I receive frequent comments on my YouTube channel from authors who relate to my past struggles, underscoring that I'm not alone in these experiences.

Looking back, I wish I had enough foresight to know my expectations weren't realistic. When breaking into the business of writing and self-publishing, you're going to find hardships, heartaches, and horse manure. Rather than hedging all your bets on simply publishing a book and making money hand over fist, diversify your author brand and prepare for the worst. I know you believe your book is amazing; otherwise, you wouldn't bother learning about being better at self-publishing.

The chances of survival for authors increase when they have more revenue-generating assets and systems. Those authors who simply publish one book on Amazon and hope it turns out for the best are asking for disappointment.

Is it okay to publish one book and go about your business? Sure! Will it yield any actual results over the short term? Possibly. Will it succeed in making money and building a brand long-term? Not likely.

One-book authors who succeed in this business are a very rare breed. If you are a one-book author, might I recommend you reconsider building out your author brand in one of the many ways previously mentioned? That way, you have more chances of winning than simply relying on one thing to keep your author brand afloat.

Analyze your mistakes if you're a writer with substantial assets and little results. Having a ton of assets doesn't mean you're entitled to winning in this business. Sure, you might have 5,000 low content books, but does that mean you deserve to earn $10,000 per month for your efforts? No. Be realistic and self-aware enough to know you're doing something wrong and need to reach out for help in your network.

To summarize how this business works:

Temper your expectations with reality.

Much like a manuscript never comes out exactly as you originally thought in your head, the story of being an author will play out way differently than you think. You must be a realist and know that the glass isn't half full or half empty; it's just a glass with liquid in it. To be less abstract, you need to view this as a business. Don't romanticize your contributions and what you think you deserve. Be real about what you achieve from the efforts you put in. Adjust course and you'll prosper over the long haul.

* * *

Reflecting on my college days and playing video games with all my dorm buddies, I realize one thing. We all had fun and built a sense of camaraderie, much in the same way we do in the self-publishing business. While I resented my roommate for winning every game with a simple yet effective button-mashing strategy, I now know that's how he enjoyed playing and winning the game. You couldn't convince me that was a cool way to do things. Now that I think about it, his strategy worked and made him happy.

Authors who pursue this business for the love and craft of writing embody the same sentiment. While they don't mind getting paid and growing readership, their biggest reason isn't *your* biggest reason. If you want to level up your self-publishing business, then you need to do more of what other people won't, so you get what they don't.

Many people will go with the adage that "Rome wasn't built in a day." This adage is highly appropriate for your self-publishing career. You're building a house one brick at a time. It's not like you can have everything prefabricated and put down all in one piece. You must build it out step-by-step, brick-by-brick, and one micro action stacked on another.

I'm sure our resident advisor, Paul, spent many countless nights and days playing his Sega Genesis. At first, he probably sucked at playing Mortal Kombat, but eventually, he saw a few small victories and learned some tricks. Once it was showtime and the guys got together, Paul could unleash his savage arsenal of moves while making the rest of us look like complete amateurs. That skill didn't come overnight, as I'm sure he spent countless hours honing his abilities to dispose of his opponents efficiently. He had to start with no skills, just like everyone else, then perfect his gaming over time.

You, too, can be like Paul. Build on the fundamental knowledge and practices you have as a self-publisher. Practice, practice, and practice some more to truly get good at the business of self-publishing. When you feel stuck, take a step back. Analyze your approach, adjust your actions, and keep pushing forward. While it'd be nice to become an overnight success, most authors don't have that luxury. Stick with it, and you'll see your breakthroughs slowly but surely.

In due time, you'll be able to not only write and publish books but make money, build your author business, and grow your author platform while doing it. Now get out there and start leveling up your author business today!

A SMALL ASK...

Now you've finished reading this book, what did you think of what you read? Were there any tips or information you found insightful? What do you think was missing from this book? While you're thinking back on what you read, it'd mean the world to me if you left an honest review on Amazon.

Reviews and ratings play a part in building relevancy for all products online. Your candid review will help other customers make an informed purchase.

Also, based on your review, I'll adjust this publication and future editions. That way, you and other indie authors can learn and grow.

Leave a review or even a rating on any of the major retailers or from where you bought this book. Thanks so much for the support!

ABOUT THE AUTHOR

Dale L. Roberts is a self-publishing advocate, award-winning author, and renowned video creator. With over 50 publications, he has become an authority in self-publishing, leading him to create his own YouTube channel, Self-Publishing with Dale, regarded as one of the premier information resources in the indie publishing community. Dale lives in Columbus, Ohio, with his wife Kelli and two rescue cats, Auggie and Allie.

RELEVANT LINKS:

- Website—SelfPublishingWithDale.com
- My Books—DaleLinks.com/MyBooks
- YouTube—YouTube.com/SelfPublishingWithDale
- YouTube Podcast—YouTube.com/@SelfPubWithDale
- Discord—DaleLinks.com/Discord
- My Email Newsletter—DaleLinks.com/SignUp
- Twitter—Twitter.com/SelfPubWithDale
- Facebook—Facebook.com/SelfPubWithDale
- Instagram—Instagram.com/SelfPubWithDale

SPECIAL THANKS

I'm infinitely grateful for all the brands and companies that have sponsored my video content. Without them, I'd have to reconsider my work as a video creator. In no order of importance, this includes Dibbly Create, Miblart, GetCovers, Fiverr, AppSumo, Findaway Voices, Lulu, North Street Book Prize, Thinkific, Kotobee, Book Award Pro, Local PR Toolkit, Archangel Ink, and…I'm sure I'm forgetting someone.

Also, big thanks to all my viewers and subscribers. Producing and publishing video content is my joy, but your successes and personal stories truly inspire me to keep doing what I'm doing. If you keep watching, I'll continue producing better content through videos, blog posts, and books like this one.

For the few viewers that hate-watch my content or leave nasty comments, thank you as well. Engagement and watch time are important metrics in building relevance through search engine algorithms. While I'm not sure why anyone would subject themselves to videos they dislike, I won't question it since it makes you happy in some capacity. You do you!

Last, an enormous thank you to my writing mentor, Jeanne De Vita. For the first seven years in this business, I wrote like a crazed lunatic, but I never truly loved the process. Your gentle ways and deep insights into writing made me rediscover the child-like wonder I had for writing. I lost that feeling back in 1995 when college sucked the joy right out of me. Fast forward to now and I simply can't go without writing in some capacity every day. The best part is I no longer feel an obligation to do it.

If you're an author looking for one of the best writing coaches for fiction and nonfiction work, get with Jeanne. She's simply the best! I put her contact details in the Additional Resources chapter.

ADDITIONAL RESOURCES

- KDP Jumpstart—DaleLinks.com/KDPJumpstart
- Universal book link generators
  - Books2Read—Books2Read.com
  - BookLinker—BookLinker.com

- For podcast interviews
  - PodcastGuests—PodcastGuests.com
  - PodMatch—PodMatch.com

- Amazon Ads Books
  - Mastering Amazon Ads by Brian Meeks—DaleLinks.com/MeeksBook1
  - Amazon Ads Unleashed by Robert Ryan—DaleLinks.com/RyanBook

- Proposal Services
  - Nusii—DaleLinks.com/Nusii
  - Quoters—Quoters.io

- Grammarly—DaleLinks.com/Grammarly
- ProWritingAid—DaleLinks.com/ProWritingAid

- My recommended reads
  - Craig Martelle's Successful Indie Author Series—DaleLinks.com/MartelleSeries
  - Chris Fox's *Write Smarter, Write Faster Series*—DaleLinks.com/FoxSeries
  - Honoree Corder's & Brian Meeks' The Prosperous Writer Series—DaleLinks.com/Prosperous

- The Self-Publishing Hub—https://TheSelfPublishingHub.com
  - The DIY Publishing Course for Beginners—https://DIYPublishing.biz

- Book Genie (Jeanne De Vita)—https://Book-Genie.com
- AwesomeGang—https://www.AwesomeGang.com
- Self-Publishing Websites:
  - Amazon Kindle Direct Publishing (KDP)—kdp.amazon.com
  - IngramSpark—ingramspark.com
  - Draft2Digital—draft2digital.com
  - PublishDrive—publishdrive.com
  - BookBaby—bookbaby.com/
  - Apple Books for Authors—authors.apple.com
  - Barnes & Noble Press—press.barnesandnoble.com
  - Kobo Writing Life—kobowritinglife.com
  - Google Play Books Partner Center—play.google.com/books/publish
  - Audiobook Creation Exchange (ACX)—acx.com
  - Findaway Voices by Spotify—findawayvoices.com
  - Author's Republic—authorsrepublic.com

REFERENCES

[i]Curcic, D. (12 January 2023). Amazon Publishing Statistics. https://wordsrated.com/amazon-publishing-statistics

[ii]Meriam-Webster, Inc. (no date). Definition of aggregate (verb). https://www.merriam-webster.com/dictionary/aggregate

[iii]Lightning Source LLC. (2 March 2023). How to Sell Your Self-Published Book to Bookstores. https://www.ingramspark.com/blog/how-to-sell-your-book-to-bookstores

[iv]Authors Guild. (27 September 2023). Key Takeaways from the Authors Guild's 2023 Author Income Survey. https://authorsguild.org/news/key-takeaways-from-2023-author-income-survey/

[v]Mohsin, M. (13 Jan 2023). 10 VIDEO MARKETING STATISTICS THAT YOU NEED TO KNOW IN 2023. https://www.oberlo.com/blog/video-marketing-statistics

www.ingramcontent.com/pod-product-compliance
Lightning Source LLC
Chambersburg PA
CBHW051259020426
42333CB00026B/3283